I Want A
Pet
Bearded Dragon

Gail Forsyth

This publication has been researched and designed to provide accurate pet care, while helping children learn the responsibilities that entail having to care for their pet bearded dragon.

Breed Profiles Publishing
Cedar City, UT 84721

Table of Contents

Note To Parents From The Author

As a parent and grandparent myself, I know the cries and wants of a child that desires a pet. When I was a child I had the same wishes to obtain just about every kind of pet I could. Every book I bought or checked out at the library was pet or animal related.

If your child has been asking for a bearded dragon, only you know if he or she is ready to take on that commitment. Your supervision will ensure that the pet is being well cared for and you'll be pleased with watching your child learn to care and nurture a pet. They may even grow up to follow a career in the pet field.

Bearded dragons can be a good choice for children. They don't require a lot of care, or any special licenses or tend to bite the mailman.

You'll find this book will help your child learn about the needs of their bearded dragon and all the while having a fun time doing it. The book has basic care topics that your child can read, plus interactive games, mazes, questions and answers, and care charts.

Childhood lasts such a short time, but the memories with a pet will last a lifetime.

Gail

Acknowledgment

I would like to acknowledge my family for all their help and words of encouragement while taking the idea for the books all the way to getting them published.

To my mother, who certainly endured some trying years when I would bring home every animal I could get my hands on.

To my children, who are a great inspiration in so much of who I am, and whose father inspired them into becoming the fine adults they are today.

To my husband, for his endless patience on the time I've spent with my own pets. It is not true that the pets eat better than he does!

A great big "Thank You" to each and every one of you.

My Pledge

Being a responsible pet owner, I understand that it takes daily care to be sure that my bearded dragon gets the care it deserves.

I pledge to give my bearded dragon food and fresh water every day.

I pledge to never abuse my bearded dragon. I will never hit my dragon.

I pledge to give my bearded dragon some out of the cage playtime as often as I can, everyday would be wonderful.

I pledge to keep my bearded dragon's cage clean.

I pledge to read books on bearded dragons, if I need to find out something about their care.

I pledge to always wash my hands after playing or cleaning up after my bearded dragon.

Signed,   Date:

_____   _____

Personal Page For Your Bearded Dragon

Your Name _____

Your Age _____

Bearded Dragon's Name _____

Bearded Dragon's Age _____

Color of Your Bearded Dragon _____

Date Obtained _____

Obtained From _____

Veterinarian _____

Paste a Picture of You and Your

Bearded Dragon Here

Always Wash Your Hands After Playing or Cleaning Up After Your Bearded Dragon
Draw Some Colorful Bubbles!

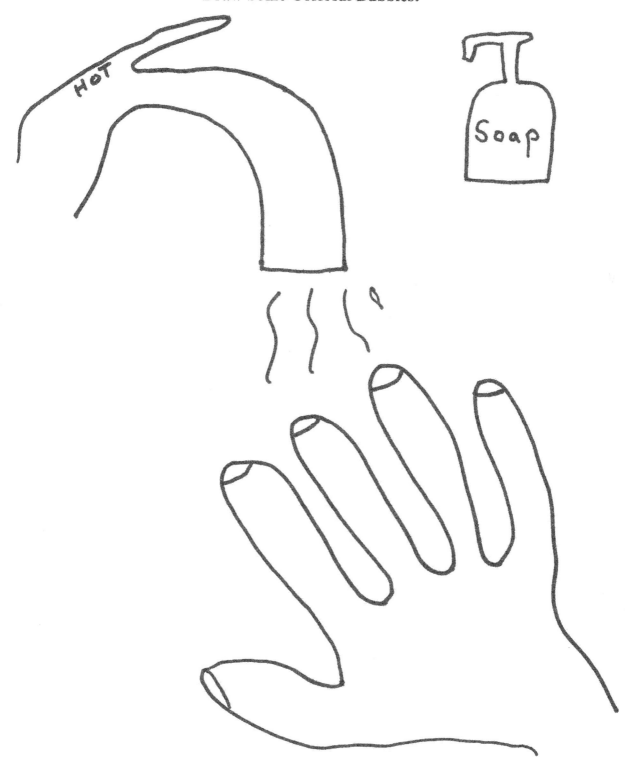

General Information on Bearded Dragons

So you've been wanting a bearded dragon for a pet. You've promised to take care of it, feed it and clean up after it. You think a bearded dragon would be fun to have as a pet. Well, I am a bearded dragon and my name is Spike. It takes more than just playing, holding and admiring my good looks to give me the proper care that I need. I'll tell you a little bit about what I like and what you'll need to do to make me happy and keep me healthy.

All in all, I am pretty easy to take care of. Just remember that all my care will fall on your shoulders. I can't get my own food, my own water or adjust the temperature to keep me comfortable. My care will have to last my whole life, each and everyday, not just for a few weeks. Are you willing to do this for me? If the answer is yes, then this book will help you to learn how to take care of me.

Here is some general information on bearded dragons. We'll discuss some of these topics in further detail in the book.

Well, you know that I am a reptile.

I am an omnivore. I eat insects, worms and some vegetables and fruits.

My life span is about 10 years.

As an adult at 2 years old, I can be about 18 to 24 inches long.

I am a social creature.

I am docile and easy to tame.

Once tame, I can ride on your shoulders.

Did you know I hatched from an egg?

I require a clean home to stay healthy.

I have little spines on the outside of my throat. These normally lay flat. If I get scared or feel threatened I'll get these spines to stand up. This makes me look bigger and more threatening.

I do have teeth.

Don't pull me up by my tail, that is not a handle.

My tail will not grow back if for some reason it gets broken off or nibbled off by another dragon or pet.

I like to climb on branches and limbs.

I like my temperature at about 80 to 85 degrees in my pen and about 95 - 100 degrees in my basking area. I need UVB lighting to bask under.

I am a very social creature. I like to interact with humans. I am normally quite docile and won't bite unless provoked or hurt.

When you first get me, go slow with me and don't make any fast movements or loud noises when you are near me. Let me get to know you. I must learn to trust you and know that you will not harm me. Putting your hand into my vivarium, which is where I live, allow me to sniff and climb onto your hand. A little wiggly food may tempt me into coming closer to you. Practice this a little each day until I am more relaxed around you. Then you can slowly take me out of my vivarium. Hold me in one hand and gently cup your other hand over my back. Let my head peek out.

When picking me up be sure to hold me securely so I don't fall. I may be a little jumpy at first, so sit close to the ground just in case I get away from you, then I won't have far to fall.

When you pick me up don't swing me in circles or throw me up in the air. Never, ever hit me. If you hit me, this will make me afraid of you and I will try to run away when you come near me. Even a slight tap can hurt me or injure me and could even cause me to die.

I do like to explore out of my vivarium. If you allow me this freedom, be sure to keep me away from electrical cords, appliances and other objects that could cause me harm. Sometimes I like to nibble on things to see if they are good to eat.

Be careful not to step on me. I am very fast. If you need to do other things and can't watch me while I explore, put me back in my vivarium for my own safety. Only take me out when you are able to keep an eye on me the whole time.

Be careful of heating vents too. I can slip into these and it will be hard for you to retrieve me.

My vivarium can keep me safe from other animals when I am in it. Once I am out and exploring, be sure that other pets are locked up in another room so that they don't hurt me. One pounce from a dog or cat can hurt me.

Some dogs and cats will except me into the household. They may just give me a sniff and pay me no attention. However, don't trust any dogs or cats around me if they are not being supervised. My tail can look like a play toy and cats are driven by instinct to pounce on things that move.

While I am out of my vivarium exploring, be extra cautious that nobody opens the door that leads out of the house. I might just slip on outside. You can hang a little sign on the door that says, "Bearded Dragon Is Loose" to warn them that I am out of my vivarium and exploring.

The next page has a handy door hanger for you to color, cut out and hang on the door. Decorate the back side of the door hanger too.

Door Hanger

Color this door hanger, cut it out and hang it on the door when I am allowed to have some free time out of my cage.

Bearded Dragon
Is
Loose

Make A Backside of the Door Hanger

Make A Backside of the Door Hanger

Questions and Answers

Here are six questions for you to answer on my basic housing and care. You will find all the answers in the previous section on General Information on Bearded Dragons. Read it as many times as you like.

How long do bearded dragons normally live? _____

Can I sleep with the cat? _____

Do I have teeth? _____

Will my tail grow back? _____

Am I docile and easy to tame? _____

Did I hatch from an egg? _____

I hope you got all the answers correct.

Word Find

Below is a word find puzzle. These words all pertain to bearded dragons, and you can find them in the section called General Information on Bearded Dragons. Circle the words and check them off the list when you find them.

___ CLEAN

___ BEARDED DRAGON

___ ACTIVE

___ REPTILE

___ SPINES

___ WATER

___ DIG

___ HIDE

___ SHELL

___ HATCHED

C	B	E	A	R	D	E	D	D	R	A	G	O	N	N	N	M	O
H	A	F	R	E	Q	E	A	R	S	K	S	W	A	T	E	R	O
A	M	F	A	C	T	I	V	E	O	R	E	F	R	A	T	S	P
T	E	R	M	G	I	C	D	O	R	E	P	T	I	L	E	S	U
C	J	I	S	Y	T	L	F	D	V	B	S	A	R	G	U	O	N
H	I	H	W	Q	S	I	A	C	D	G	C	D	I	G	B	S	J
E	U	G	U	I	N	M	A	D	I	G	J	W	F	A	Z	X	X
D	M	T	M	V	K	B	J	Q	W	R	O	D	E	N	T	T	Y
S	P	I	N	E	S	U	L	A	N	W	C	L	E	V	E	R	W
S	H	E	L	L	S	B	C	A	X	S	Z	O	A	H	I	D	E

Draw Me Some Spines

My Vivarium

My pen is very important as this is where I'll spend the majority of my time. It will keep me safe and give me a home of my own. My home is called a vivarium or some people just call it a tank if it is made of glass.

When buying my tank you'll be able to see lots of them at the pet store to make your decision as to which one you want. Some people like glass tanks and others like a wire cage. Which ever one you decide on try to get me the biggest one you can. I will grow fast.

You'll have to take into account the space that you have at home where my tank will be sitting. You might also want to be able to move my tank from different locations. So you'll want to get one that you can handle and transport easily. Some people like to get two pens, one for my main home and a small pen or crate for taking me to the veterinarian, a short car ride, to take me outdoors or for taking me back to the pet store to pick out a new tasty treat with you.

The small pen or crate can also be used to put me in while you are giving my big main vivarium a thorough cleaning. This will keep me from slipping away and getting lost or hurt.

Do not set my vivarium in direct sunlight that is coming through a window. This will make my home too hot for me. I like the temperature between 80 – 85 degrees and a little warmer right where I bask at 95 – 100 degrees. My nighttime temperature can be no lower than about 65 – 70 degrees. It is best to use a thermometer so that you are sure how hot or cold my home is. Check it often to keep me comfortable.

Don't leave the thermometer in my vivarium where I could bite and break it.

Be careful what you set my pen next to. If I am too close to your curtains, cords, plants, books or other objects, I just might try to pull those into my pen and see if they are good things to eat. I'm sure you don't want to tell your teacher that your bearded dragon ate your homework.

My vivarium should be completely enclosed with a lid. Most glass tanks come with a lid. Some have light bulbs and sockets to light the vivarium up.

I will also need a UVB light. Hang this light right over my favorite basking area.

Bearded dragons like places to hide. It also helps us cool off if we get too hot. So I would appreciate some hiding caves or logs in my pen as well.

Keep my pen at one end slightly cooler than at the other. Then I can move around as I need to stay comfortable. You can even put a under tank heater on one end to warm that end up.

We like to climb on branches and limbs and to scamper over rocks. Check all items to be sure they are sturdy and won't come falling down on me.

I also will need a small heavy dish for my drinking water. You can buy some at the pet store that look like a rock with a little spot for my water. Change my water everyday.

A nice flat dish or plate will work fine for my salads.

That should do it for my basic living arrangements. I don't need too much but setting my pen up correctly will keep me happy, healthy and safe.

Lighting

Bearded dragons love to bask in the sun or under a light.

The correct type of light to have in my vivarium will be one that offers the UVB rays. You can find these lights at the pet store.

When you are buying my vivarium, many of them will come with a light bulb socket right in the hood of the vivarium. If it comes with a bulb, ask the store attendant if the bulb is UVB. Most often they are just for lighting up my tank and will add a little heat to my home. Which is nice.

I like my temperature to be about 80 – 85 degrees. Under my favorite basking area where the UVB bulb should be shining down on, I like the temperature to be around 95 – 100 degrees. At night don't let my vivarium drop below 65 – 70 degrees. If the room that my vivarium sits in is cold, you can add a under the tank heater to help warm my home up.

Proper UVB lighting is essential for my bones and helps me digest my food. It helps me to produce vitamin D which helps me to use the calcium that I need.

You can take me outside to allow me to get some natural sunshine. You will need to be sure I have a shady spot to retreat to, in case it gets too hot, and give me a little dish of cool water to drink too.

About 8 to 14 hours a day is needed if using a UVB bulb. Put this bulb right over my favorite basking area, about 8 inches above from where I normally bask.

This lighting is very important to my health.

Healthy Foods For Bearded Dragons

Keeping me healthy with proper nutrition is not too hard. I am an omnivore, which means I'll eat insects, worms and some vegetables and fruit.

When I am a baby feed me small pieces that are easy for me to eat. Offer me insects about twice a day. Let me eat for about 10 minutes. Dust the insects with some calcium powder right before feeding me them.

Crickets can also be gut loaded before feeding them to me. This is where the cricket will eat a very nutritious meal, then when I eat the cricket that nutrition is passed onto me.

For adult bearded dragons you can feed me some insects about once a day. Feed me as many as I will eat in about a 10 minute period. These insects should also be dusted with calcium, just like for baby bearded dragons.

You can also make me a good salad with any of the following fruits and vegetables. Change the salad each day. I don't like old moldy food and it is not healthy for me to eat.

Here are some tasty items to add to my salad.

Grated carrots
Squash
Green leafy vegetables
Turnip greens
Beet greens
Blueberries
Bananas
Dandelion greens
Carrot tops
Green peppers

I eat a large amount of insects and other small creatures. Try to give me as much of a varied diet as you can. This will ensure that I am getting the vitamins and minerals that I need. It also keeps meal time interesting for me.

Here are some of my favorite insects and worms.

Crickets
Meal worms
Wax worms
Silk worms
Grasshoppers
Katydids
Beetles

Be sure my vivarium and me are warmed up before feeding me. The heat helps with my digestion of food.

Feeding is an important part of my day. I'll learn to recognize you and you'll notice that I'm quite happy when you come to feed me.

What Not To Feed Your Bearded Dragon

Some plants and bugs should not be fed to your Bearded Dragon. Here is a list of things that I should not eat. Please take care of me and don't feed me these foods, bugs or plants. Many will make me ill and possibly kill me.

Corn cobs
Oleander
Chocolate
Soda Pop
Mushrooms
Fireflies
Box Elder Bugs
Poinsettia
Mistletoe
Caffeine
Bird seed

Many house plants are not good for me. So check to be sure that I can eat them, or just avoid giving me any of them.

Vitamins & Minerals

Bearded dragons should have calcium dusted over some of their crickets before letting me eat them. An easy way to do this is to put a few crickets in a small jar with a lid. Add the calcium and shake it up. Then feed the crickets to me.

If you are feeding me a good well-balanced diet, I may not need any extra vitamins and minerals unless I have been sick for some reason.

If I have been ill, your veterinarian will instruct you on how to give me any extra vitamins or minerals to make me better.

Never feed me your vitamins. Those are for people and they could make me very sick.

I know you are aware that I do need clean water to drink everyday and I appreciate you taking care of that for me.

Questions and Answers on Food

Here are a few questions for you to answer on what foods to feed me and what foods I should not eat.

What foods will make up my main diet? _____

Can I eat Box Elder Bugs? _____

Can I eat worms? _____

Should I have soda pop? _____

Chocolate sure smells good. Can I eat chocolate? _____

Can you name a plant that is not good for me? _____

I hope you got these questions correct.

Food is an important part of my day. Eating the correct foods will keep me happy and healthy. I know you are in charge of feeding me correctly.

Substrate

A substrate is basically what the floor of the vivarium will have on it.

For baby bearded dragons sand is not recommended. They will eat the sand while they are eating their live insects. The sand can block their intestines and cause problems. For the same reason, you do not want to use wood shavings or walnut shells.

Some older bearded dragons can use sand if it is the kind that is used for a child's sandbox.

Don't use sand or dirt from the desert or the woods. This could have ticks or lice in it and you won't want to introduce that to your bearded dragon.

Many bearded dragon owners like to use either plain paper towels or even heavy floor tiles as the substrate. A rubber mat is also a good choice. The tiles and mats can easily be cleaned. The paper towels can just be disposed of in the trash once they become wet or dirty.

To make the vivarium look more natural you could also put down a large piece of indoor – outdoor carpeting. Brown or green would look nice. This can also be taken outside and hosed off when it becomes dirty.

If you choose the indoor – outdoor carpeting, cut two pieces for the vivarium. This way one can be drying and you can put the other clean one in my cage.

Grooming

Well, you can put away the brush and comb. I won't be needing them.

My grooming is very easy.

The most help I'll need from you is to take a good look at my toenails.

If they are starting to get too long, they will need to be trimmed.
Have the pet store or your veterinarian show you how to do this.

The pet store will have special toenail clippers made especially for pets.

Check over my body for any cuts, scrapes or sores. Sometimes I might injure myself while hurrying to get an insect in my cage.

Bearded dragons will even get in a little shallow dish of water to take a bath. Don't make the water deep. We can't swim that well. We also enjoy just a little spritz of warm water on us. Spritz me outside of my vivarium. Otherwise, you may get my home too wet and that will cause a rise in humidity.

Check me over for any mites on my body. These are little bugs that you will want to get off of me. Check with the pet store for a good remedy to rid me of mites. Don't use dog or cat flea powders or spray on me.

Mites are very tiny, so use a magnifying glass to see if I have them. Sometimes you will see mites floating in my water.

Group of 3 Bearded Dragons to Color

Shedding

Being a reptile, I do shed my skin.

This will happen quite often as I grow.

It is a normal process. When you see the old dead skin on me, don't try to pull it off.

It is better if I shed this skin myself. You will see me rubbing on my rocks and any branches in my vivarium. This will help me get the loose skin off.

If bearded dragons are having trouble shedding their skin it could be caused from a couple of different reasons.

The first reason would be from lack of a good diet. The second reason may be from poor lighting in my vivarium.

Both food and UVB lighting are so important to my health.

Check me over for mites too. These little creatures will suck my blood and cause me to not shed my skin properly.

If my dead skin is not coming off and I look stressed or listless, have me checked over by my veterinarian or someone at the pet store.

Play Table

Having a play table is a lot of fun. It is basically a nice play area for me to explore and for you to observe me, without having me loose exploring through your house or room.

Play tables have sides high enough so I can't crawl over them, or the table can be enclosed for greater safety. This will prevent me from walking off the table and getting hurt. You can make a play table or buy one. You might even construct one out of a large cardboard box. This can be our very own little hideaway.

Play tables are also great for when the weather gets cold outside and I am stuck in the house. It makes my days fun and I won't get bored from being in my vivarium all day and night.

My table is a good place for me to walk around, climb and interact with you. Add some branches for me to climb on. I'll need some lighting and of course a few places to hide under.

This is a good time for me to take a little bath. Give me a shallow dish of warm water to slip into. Do not use any soap or bubbles on me. Dry me off gently with a soft towel before putting me back into my vivarium.

Put down some brown craft paper or butcher paper. This is easy to dispose of if I happen to use the restroom on it, or if I get it wet after climbing out of my bath water. You can even use old newspaper, but watch me close to be sure I don't try to eat it.

This is a good time for you to check me over for any problems. Look at my feet, my tail and my spines. See if there are any cuts, scratches or sores on me. Are my eyes clear? Do I have a runny nose? How about any of those nasty mites? Spotting these ailments while they are small is easier to remedy and fix.

Be careful of any cats or dogs that may try to jump onto the play table to get me. Especially if the play table doesn't have a lid or cover.

Keep an eye on me as I like to hide.

Special treats just for when we are playing on the table together would be a good idea. I'll learn to enjoy the table and look forward to having you come and get me out of my vivarium.

These outings are fun and they will make me blissfully tired and glad that I am your bearded dragon.

Taking Your Bearded Dragon Outdoors

Bearded dragons enjoy the outdoors. The heat from the sun feels good and is very good for me. Bearded dragons like to bask in the sun.

Be sure that I have some shade from the sun if you are letting me walk around. If I am going to be outdoors for a long time, I will need some cool water to drink.

When taking me outdoors be aware of any dangers that might be there.

Make sure I can't walk into a pond, creek, lake or ocean. I can swim but not that well. Fast currents might take me away.

Keep a close eye on me to see what I am chewing on. Watch for cut pieces of glass, plastics, balloons, nails, rocks and other things that you know are not good for me to eat. Bearded dragons may pick up anything to see if it tastes good.

Any loose dogs or cats in the area may try to get me. Keep a close watch for them.

Be aware of any birds of prey that you have in your area. Eagles, falcons, hawks and even owls. As well as wild coyotes, foxes, raccoons, skunks and even large snakes.

If you see any danger in the area, it would be best to take me back indoors to my safe vivarium or to my play table.

Making a safe outdoor area which would be completely enclosed would be great. Then I can walk and explore and enjoy the sun and my outing.

Be aware that some animals will try to dig under my enclosed pen. The best way to know that I am safe is for you to stay with me while I am out roaming and enjoying myself. Pull up a chair and watch me. I am very entertaining and would love to make you smile.

Bearded Dragon Maze

Bearded Dragons like worms. Can you take a red crayon and help this hungry bearded dragon find the worm through the maze? Then will you take an orange crayon and help him find the cricket?

Bearded Dragon

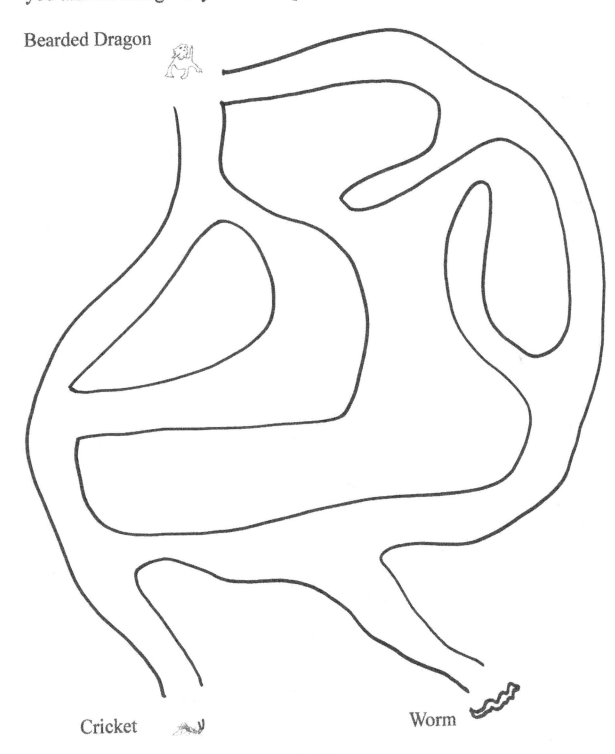

Cricket

Worm

Color Me

Hibernation

Bearded dragons don't hibernate. They go through a process similar to hibernation, but it is called brumation.

During this time, which often takes place in late fall, you'll see your bearded dragon become rather listless.

You'll see it sleeping more and eating less.

The times for this brumation will vary. Some bearded dragons will sleep for just a day or two. Others will sleep for a month.

Keep my vivarium tank warm as usual. Keep my lights on as well. I may not eat any insects at this time, but try to keep me a little salad in my vivarium just in case I do get hungry and need to keep my energy up.

You'll miss me during these times, but just let me be. I won't be active and trying to play with me can stress me out.

This will soon pass and I'll be back to my old normal self before you know it.

Your bearded dragon may never go into brumation. Every dragon has their own time table on when and if they will choose to go into brumation.

Captive Bred Bearded Dragons

Chances are you will be getting your bearded dragon that has been captive bred, and not caught in the wild.

The best place to purchase your bearded dragon will be from either a breeder or a pet store.

These places will also be able to tell you about how old your new bearded dragon is, what it has been eating, how friendly it is and they will be able to answer all of your questions about your bearded dragon.

It is not a good idea to take wild bearded dragons out of their natural habitat and try to make them into a pet.

Wild bearded dragons are much more skittish and afraid of humans. Many wild bearded dragons are protected by laws so that they are not captured from their wild habitats.

Captive bred bearded dragons are more used to humans. Being bred in captivity they have been accustomed to getting their food from humans. These dragons make much better pets.

Once a bearded dragon has been bred in captivity, it should also never be turned loose into the wild. This is also against the law in many places.

Many captive bred bearded dragons will die if turned loose into the wild.

Health Issues For Bearded Dragons

Bearded dragons can have a few health issues.

I'll list a few things here. If you feel your dragon needs to see a veterinarian don't hesitate to make an appointment and have him checked over.

Mites are a problem that many reptiles get. They will infest me as well. They are very tiny bugs and hard to see. Using a magnifying glass will help you spot them on me or you may even see them in my drinking water.

Mites are hard to get rid of and you'll need to clean my vivarium and all my logs, dishes, rocks, and branches. Along with getting me some special mite medicine at the pet store.

Another health issue is a lack of calcium in my diet. I need calcium in order to stay healthy.

Some bearded dragons may get internal parasites. Your veterinarian can check to see if this is a problem with your bearded dragon.

Sometimes we may get impacted in our digestive system. This can be caused by eating sand or gravel or from eating insects that are too large for me to eat easily.

We can get fungus and bacterial skin infections if our vivarium is kept too wet.

Respiratory infections can be caused by drafts.

I am normally pretty hardy and by feeding me the right foods and keeping me the right temperature will help ward off many health concerns.

Missing Vowels

Here are more puzzles that you can do. Fill in the missing vowels from the words below. Some of the words pertain to what bearded dragons like to eat and do, and the last two words are what your dragon should have plenty of when he is outside.

Use these vowels: A – E – I – O – U

B _ _ RD _ D   DR _ G _ N

SH _ D

CR _ WL

SL _ TH _ R

B _ SK

_ _ T

T _ NG _ _

H _ D _

SK _ N

SL _ _ P

C _ G _

W _ RMS

SH _ D _

W _ T _ R

Word Find

Below is a word find puzzle. Can you find the following words in the puzzle? Circle the words and check them off the list when you find them.

___ BEARDED DRAGON

___ CAGE

___ SKIN

___ TAIL

___ CLAWS

___ TONGUE

___ SUNSHINE

___ SHADE

___ HIDE

___ WATER

___ SHED

___ FOOD

B	N	D	V	F	O	O	D	R	P	F	A	S	M	M	H	I	D	E	Z
M	H	S	R	A	C	B	I	T	S	B	F	U	R	A	W	A	T	R	E
U	S	A	A	G	H	J	U	M	P	E	E	N	C	T	A	M	S	A	Q
S	K	I	N	E	W	F	R	U	P	V	A	S	S	T	T	W	A	T	E
I	E	M	P	P	L	E	M	H	O	V	S	H	A	D	E	E	H	O	B
S	D	O	X	I	O	P	R	R	A	C	C	I	A	S	R	J	H	N	P
H	A	N	S	J	E	R	T	Y	U	B	I	N	N	Y	B	A	B	G	J
E	H	O	P	V	B	V	C	A	E	A	S	E	R	S	U	N	N	U	R
D	I	T	N	T	G	H	K	A	C	A	R	R	B	Y	W	R.	X	E	O
B	J	U	P	P	Y	O	L	O	V	U	W	A	T	A	I	L	S	I	N
B	C	L	A	W	S	R	B	E	A	R	D	E	D	D	R	A	G	O	N

Color Me

Daily Care Chart

Below is a chart to help you remember to take care of your pet bearded dragon.

You may want to make some copies of the chart, before you start to use it. Then you'll have plenty for the year and you can hang it someplace where you'll see it to remind you about my daily care.

Put a little smiley face, star or check mark each time you have taken care of my needs.

Keeping me properly fed and clean will make me happy and healthy.

Be sure to clean the area outside of my cage too. Just in case I've kicked some waste, bedding or food out. This will prevent ants and other bugs from coming, and help to control any odors.

	Sunday	Monday	Tuesday	Wednesday	Thursday	Friday	Saturday
Feeding							
Watering							
Playtime							
Clean Daily							
Clean Weekly							

Make Your Own Note Cards

On the next page you will find two different pictures for you to make your own note cards.

Carefully tear the page out of your book. Cut on the dotted line and trim the edge that was torn out of your book.

Fold the paper in half.

Color the pictures and add any flowers, trees, clouds, the sun, etc.

Add your own wording on the inside, such as, Happy Birthday, Get Well Soon or whatever else you'd like.

Give the note card to someone special.

Made For You By:

Made For You By:

40

Make Your Own Bookmark

Below are three bookmarks. Cut out and draw your own Bearded Dragon on one end and color them in nice bright colors for your books. If you cover them with clear mailing tape, it will make them sturdy.

I Love My Bearded Dragon!

I Love My Bearded Dragon!

I Love My Bearded Dragon!

After you cut out your bookmarks, draw or write your name on the back sides before covering them with tape.

Other Books in the Series

When you need other animal care books with fun activities, ask for these books from your favorite bookseller.

I Want A Pet Chinchilla	ISBN: 978-1491274415
I Want A Pet Hamster	ISBN: 978-1491274286
I Want A Pet Rabbit	ISBN: 978-1491273630
I Want A Pet Guinea Pig	ISBN: 978-1491273968
I Want A Pet Ferret	ISBN: 978-1491274118
I Want A Pet Rat	ISBN: 978-1491274224
I Want A Pet Tortoise	ISBN: 978-1492303275
I Want A Pet Turtle	ISBN: 978-1492303312
I Want A Pet Parakeet	ISBN: 978-1492303350
I Want A Pet Parrot	ISBN: 978-1492303398
I Want A Pet Cockatiel	ISBN: 978-1492303435
I Want A Pet Iguana	ISBN: 978-1492303473
I Want A Pet Bearded Dragon	ISBN: 978-1492303541
I Want A Pet Chameleon	ISBN: 978-1492303633
I Want A Pet Gecko	ISBN: 978-1492303701
I Want A Pet Lizard	ISBN: 978-1492303732
I Want A Pet Snake	ISBN: 978-1492303800
I Want A Pet Betta	ISBN: 978-1492303855
I Want A Kitten	ISBN: 978-1492303886
I Want A Puppy	ISBN: 978-1492303916
I Want A Pony	ISBN: 978-1492303954

26447751R00030

Made in the USA
San Bernardino, CA
29 November 2015